This Book Belongs To:

Introduction

Why Self-Care Is Important:

Self-care is about giving ourselves relief when we feel overwhelmed. Many women have so much responsibility in their daily lives they forget to take care of their own personal needs. When the focus is always on providing care for others you put yourself at risk for low self-esteem, deeper levels of unhappiness, and feelings of resentment. You are also in danger of burning out and therefore will be unable to continue to provide the necessary level of care to all who depend on you to be there for them.

Self-Care Is NOT Indulgent:

Taking time out to care for yourself can remind you and others that you and your needs are important, too. Feeling your best both physically and emotionally makes you more resilient and able to manage life's daily stress in a more positive way.

Choosing Self-Care Activities:

Self-care is a personal matter and everyone's approach will be different. An activity that one person finds soothing and relaxing can irritate and annoy another person. It is important that you identify activities and practices that support your wellbeing and help you to maintain positive self-care.

Self-Care Activity Suggestions:

Take a Nap
Visit a Friend
Practice Mindfulness
Start a Gratitude Journal
Practice Deep Breathing
Meditation
Yoga
Spend Time in Nature
Crafting
Hiking
Read for Fun
Learn a New Dance
Take a Break from Your Cell Phone
Go to the Movies
Play a Sport
Hire Someone to Clean Your House
Unfriend Toxic People

Do a Routine Differently
Sew, Quilt or Knit
Write a Limerick or Haiku
Rearrange Furniture
Learn a New Board Game
Try Adult Coloring
Listen to a Podcast
Do an Online Tutorial
Unplug from Social Media
Play an Instrument
Visit the Library
Have a Spa Day
Work on a Jigsaw Puzzle
Listen to an Audio Book
Have a Cathartic Cry
Set 3 Goals Daily
Take a Bubble Bath

My A-Z of Self-Care Ideas

A

B

C

D

E

F

G

H

I

J

K

L

M

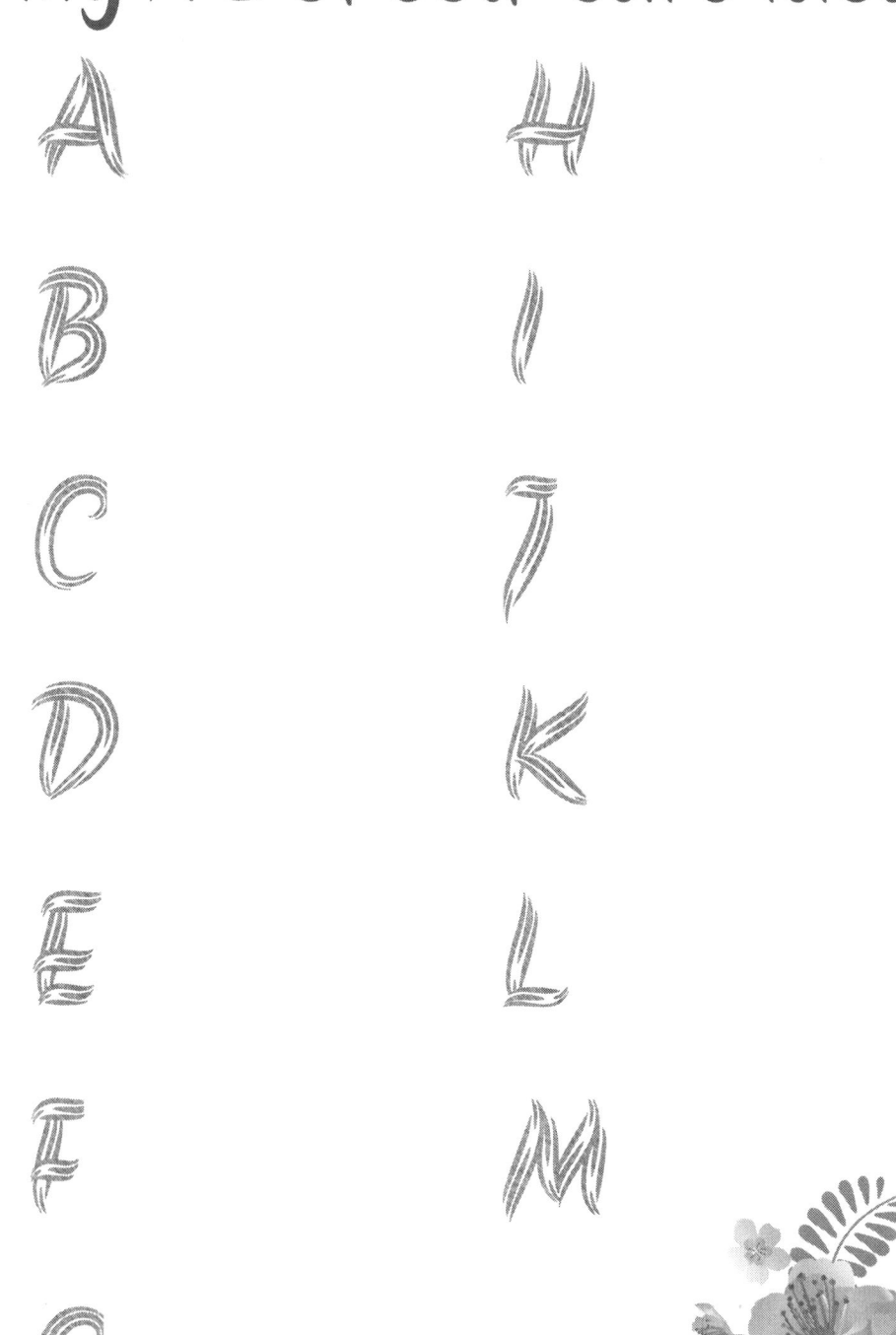

Think of a self-care activity that starts with each letter of the alphabet

N   U

O   V

P   W

Q   X

R   Y

S   Z

T

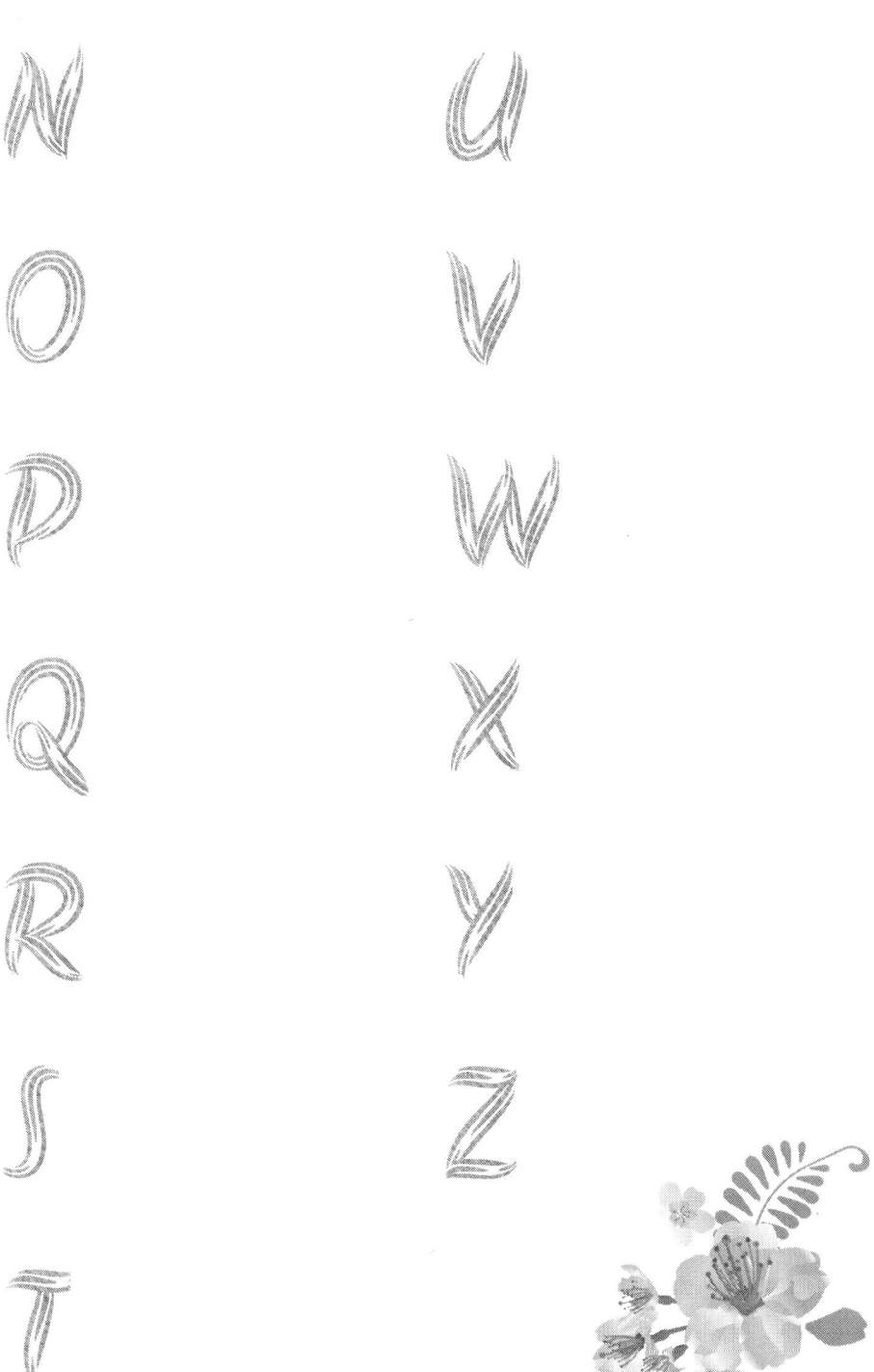

Planning My 30 days of Self-Care

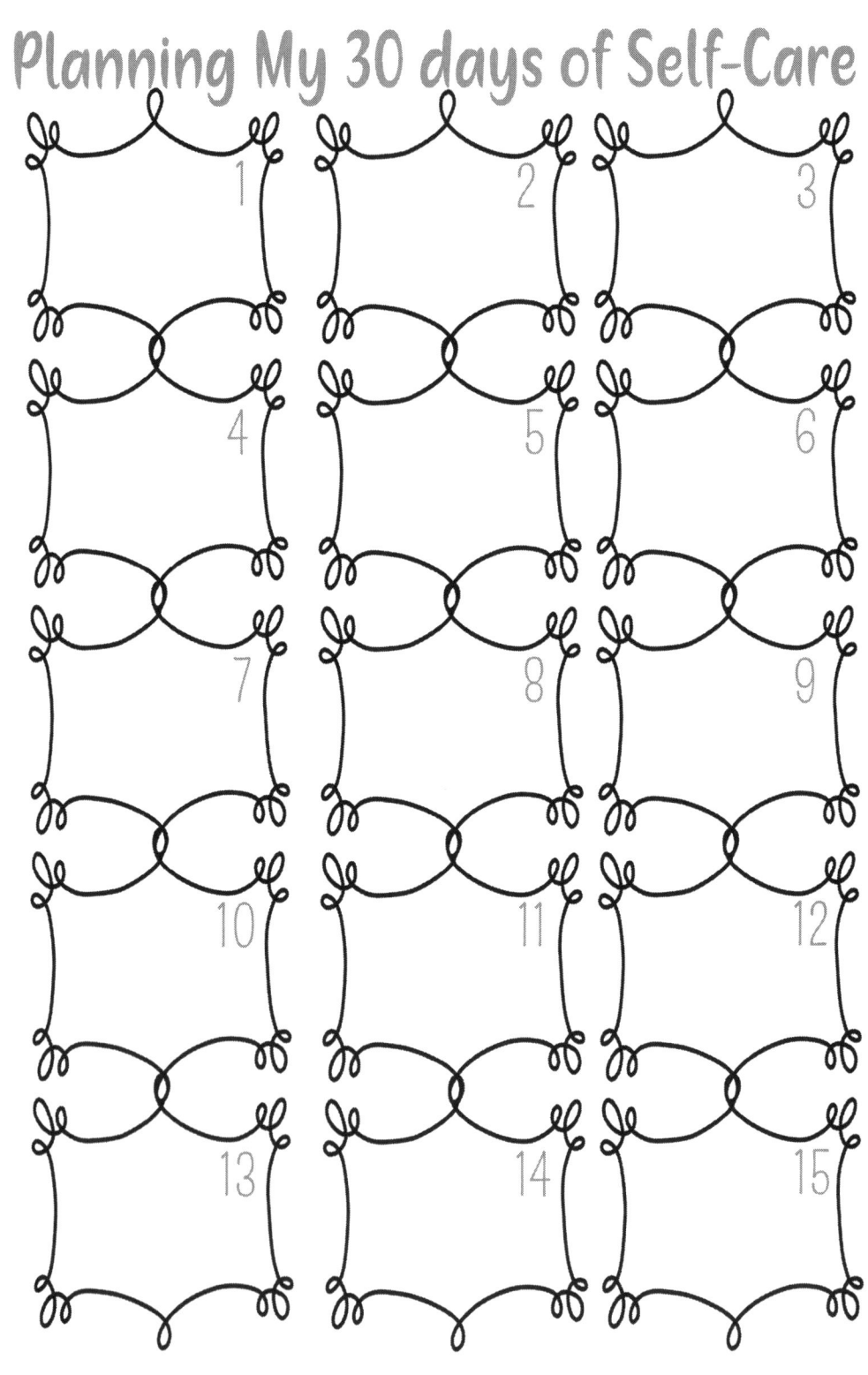

Try and plan as many self-care activities for the next 30 days as possible

Day One

Date: ....

Today's self-care activity: ....

How do you feel today?

What did today bring for you?

How did you deal with any challenges that came your way?

I am...	My Day	
	General mood:	☆ ☆ ☆ ☆ ☆
	Hydration:	○ ○ ○ ○ ○ ○ ○ ○
	Sleep:	Z Z Z Z Z Z Z
	Energy Levels:	✦ ✦ ✦ ✦ ✦ ✦ ✦ ✦ ✦

Describe in detail what you got from doing today's
self-care activity

_____

_____

_____

_____

_____

_____

What would you like tomorrow to bring for you?

_____

_____

_____

Day Two

Date: ....

Today's self-care activity: ....

How do you feel today?

_____

_____

_____

 What did today bring for you?

_____

_____

_____

_____

How did you deal with any challenges that came your way?

_____

_____

_____

_____

_____

I am...	My Day	
	General mood:	☆ ☆ ☆ ☆ ☆
	Hydration:	○ ○ ○ ○ ○ ○ ○ ○
	Sleep:	Z Z Z Z Z Z Z
	Energy Levels:	✦ ✦ ✦ ✦ ✦ ✦ ✦ ✦

Describe in detail what you got from doing today's
self-care activity

_____

_____

_____

_____

_____

_____

_____

What would you like tomorrow to bring for you?

_____

_____

_____

Day Three

Date: _____

Today's self-care activity: _____

How do you feel today?

 What did today bring for you?

_____

_____

_____

_____

How did you deal with any challenges that came your way?

_____

_____

_____

_____

I am...	My Day	
	General mood:	☆ ☆ ☆ ☆ ☆
	Hydration:	○ ○ ○ ○ ○ ○ ○ ○
	Sleep:	ZZZZZZZZ
	Energy Levels:	✢ ✢ ✢ ✢ ✢ ✢ ✢ ✢

Describe in detail what you got from doing today's self-care activity

_____

_____

_____

_____

_____

_____

_____

What would you like tomorrow to bring for you?

_____

_____

_____

Day Four

Date: _____

Today's self-care activity: _____

How do you feel today?

 What did today bring for you?

_____

_____

_____

_____

How did you deal with any challenges that came your way?

_____

_____

_____

_____

_____

I am...	**My Day**	
	General mood:	☆ ☆ ☆ ☆ ☆
	Hydration:	○ ○ ○ ○ ○ ○ ○ ○
	Sleep:	Z Z Z Z Z Z Z
	Energy Levels:	✦ ✦ ✦ ✦ ✦ ✦ ✦ ✦

Describe in detail what you got from doing today's self-care activity

_____

_____

_____

_____

_____

_____

_____

What would you like tomorrow to bring for you?

_____

_____

_____

Day Five

Date: _____

Today's self-care activity: _____

> ## How do you feel today?
>
> _____
> _____
> _____

 What did today bring for you?

_____
_____
_____
_____

How did you deal with any challenges that came your way?

_____
_____
_____
_____
_____

I am...	My Day	
	General mood:	☆ ☆ ☆ ☆ ☆
	Hydration:	○ ○ ○ ○ ○ ○ ○ ○
	Sleep:	Z Z Z Z Z Z Z
	Energy Levels:	✛ ✛ ✛ ✛ ✛ ✛ ✛ ✛

Describe in detail what you got from doing today's self-care activity

_____

_____

_____

_____

_____

_____

What would you like tomorrow to bring for you?

_____

_____

_____

_____

Day Six

Today's self-care activity:

How do you feel today?

What did today bring for you?

How did you deal with any challenges that came your way?

I am...

My Day

General mood:	☆ ☆ ☆ ☆ ☆
Hydration:	○ ○ ○ ○ ○ ○ ○
Sleep:	Z Z Z Z Z Z Z Z
Energy Levels:	✦ ✦ ✦ ✦ ✦ ✦ ✦ ✦

Describe in detail what you got from doing today's
self-care activity

_____

_____

_____

_____

_____

_____

_____

What would you like tomorrow to bring for you?

_____

_____

_____

Day Seven

Date: _____

Today's self-care activity: _____

How do you feel today?

_____
_____
_____

What did today bring for you?

_____
_____
_____
_____

How did you deal with any challenges that came your way?

_____
_____
_____
_____

I am...	My Day	
	General mood:	☆ ☆ ☆ ☆ ☆
	Hydration:	○ ○ ○ ○ ○ ○ ○
	Sleep:	Z Z Z Z Z Z Z
	Energy Levels:	✦ ✦ ✦ ✦ ✦ ✦ ✦

Describe in detail what you got from doing today's self-care activity

_____

_____

_____

_____

_____

_____

What would you like tomorrow to bring for you?

_____

_____

_____

Day Eight

Date: _____

Today's self-care activity: _____

How do you feel today?

_____

_____

_____

What did today bring for you?

_____

_____

_____

How did you deal with any challenges that came your way?

_____

_____

_____

_____

I am...	My Day	
	General mood:	☆ ☆ ☆ ☆ ☆
	Hydration:	○ ○ ○ ○ ○ ○ ○ ○
	Sleep:	Z Z Z Z Z Z Z
	Energy Levels:	✤ ✤ ✤ ✤ ✤ ✤ ✤ ✤ ✤

Describe in detail what you got from doing today's
self-care activity

_____

_____

_____

_____

_____

_____

_____

What would you like tomorrow to bring for you?

_____

_____

_____

Day Nine

Date: _____

Today's self-care activity: _____

How do you feel today?

 What did today bring for you?

_____

_____

_____

_____

How did you deal with any challenges that came your way?

_____

_____

_____

_____

I am...	My Day	
	General mood:	☆ ☆ ☆ ☆ ☆
	Hydration:	○ ○ ○ ○ ○ ○ ○ ○
	Sleep:	Z Z Z Z Z Z Z
	Energy Levels:	✦ ✦ ✦ ✦ ✦ ✦ ✦ ✦

Describe in detail what you got from doing today's
self-care activity

_____

_____

_____

_____

_____

_____

_____

What would you like tomorrow to bring for you?

_____

_____

_____

_____

Day Ten

Date: _____

Today's self-care activity: _____

> ## How do you feel today?
>
> _____
>
> _____
>
> _____

 What did today bring for you?

_____

_____

_____

_____

How did you deal with any challenges that came your way?

_____

_____

_____

_____

_____

I am...

My Day

General mood:	☆ ☆ ☆ ☆ ☆
Hydration:	○ ○ ○ ○ ○ ○ ○ ○
Sleep:	ZZZZZZZ
Energy Levels:	✛✛✛✛✛✛✛✛

Describe in detail what you got from doing today's
self-care activity

_____

_____

_____

_____

_____

_____

_____

What would you like tomorrow to bring for you?

_____

_____

_____

Day Eleven

Date:

Today's self-care activity:

How do you feel today?

 What did today bring for you?

How did you deal with any challenges that came your way?

I am...	My Day	
	General mood:	☆ ☆ ☆ ☆ ☆
	Hydration:	○ ○ ○ ○ ○ ○ ○ ○
	Sleep:	Z Z Z Z Z Z Z
	Energy Levels:	✦ ✦ ✦ ✦ ✦ ✦ ✦ ✦

Describe in detail what you got from doing today's
self-care activity

_____

_____

_____

_____

_____

_____

What would you like tomorrow to bring for you?

_____

_____

_____

Day Twelve

Date: _____

Today's self-care activity: _____

How do you feel today?

 What did today bring for you?

_____

_____

_____

_____

How did you deal with any challenges that came your way?

_____

_____

_____

_____

I am...	My Day	
	General mood:	☆ ☆ ☆ ☆ ☆
	Hydration:	○ ○ ○ ○ ○ ○ ○ ○
	Sleep:	Z Z Z Z Z Z Z
	Energy Levels:	✛ ✛ ✛ ✛ ✛ ✛ ✛ ✛

Describe in detail what you got from doing today's
self-care activity

_____

_____

_____

_____

_____

_____

What would you like tomorrow to bring for you?

_____

_____

_____

Day Thirteen

Today's self-care activity:

How do you feel today?

 What did today bring for you?

How did you deal with any challenges that came your way?

I am...	My Day	
	General mood:	☆ ☆ ☆ ☆ ☆
	Hydration:	○ ○ ○ ○ ○ ○ ○ ○
	Sleep:	Z Z Z Z Z Z Z Z
	Energy Levels:	✚ ✚ ✚ ✚ ✚ ✚ ✚ ✚

Describe in detail what you got from doing today's self-care activity

_____

_____

_____

_____

_____

_____

What would you like tomorrow to bring for you?

_____

_____

_____

Day Fourteen

Date: _____

Today's self-care activity: _____

How do you feel today?

_____
_____
_____

 What did today bring for you?

_____
_____
_____
_____

How did you deal with any challenges that came your way?

_____
_____
_____
_____
_____

I am...	My Day	
	General mood:	☆ ☆ ☆ ☆ ☆
	Hydration:	○ ○ ○ ○ ○ ○ ○ ○
	Sleep:	Z Z Z Z Z Z Z
	Energy Levels:	✛ ✛ ✛ ✛ ✛ ✛ ✛ ✛

Describe in detail what you got from doing today's
self-care activity

_____

_____

_____

_____

_____

_____

What would you like tomorrow to bring for you?

_____

_____

_____

Day Fifteen

Today's self-care activity:

How do you feel today?

 What did today bring for you?

How did you deal with any challenges that came your way?

I am...	My Day	
	General mood:	☆ ☆ ☆ ☆ ☆
	Hydration:	○ ○ ○ ○ ○ ○ ○ ○
	Sleep:	Z Z Z Z Z Z Z Z
	Energy Levels:	✦ ✦ ✦ ✦ ✦ ✦ ✦ ✦

Describe in detail what you got from doing today's self-care activity

_____

_____

_____

_____

_____

_____

_____

What would you like tomorrow to bring for you?

_____

_____

_____

Day Sixteen

Today's self-care activity:_____

How do you feel today?

What did today bring for you?

How did you deal with any challenges that came your way?

I am...	My Day	
	General mood:	☆ ☆ ☆ ☆ ☆
	Hydration:	○ ○ ○ ○ ○ ○ ○ ○
	Sleep:	Z Z Z Z Z Z Z
	Energy Levels:	✚ ✚ ✚ ✚ ✚ ✚ ✚

Describe in detail what you got from doing today's self-care activity

_____

_____

_____

_____

_____

_____

_____

What would you like tomorrow to bring for you?

_____

_____

_____

Day Seventeen

Today's self-care activity:

How do you feel today?

 What did today bring for you?

How did you deal with any challenges that came your way?

I am...	My Day	
	General mood:	☆ ☆ ☆ ☆ ☆
	Hydration:	○ ○ ○ ○ ○ ○ ○
	Sleep:	Z Z Z Z Z Z Z
	Energy Levels:	✦ ✦ ✦ ✦ ✦ ✦ ✦

Describe in detail what you got from doing today's
self-care activity

_____

_____

_____

_____

_____

_____

_____

What would you like tomorrow to bring for you?

_____

_____

_____

_____

Day Eighteen

Today's self-care activity:

How do you feel today?

What did today bring for you?

How did you deal with any challenges that came your way?

I am...	My Day	
	General mood:	☆ ☆ ☆ ☆ ☆
	Hydration:	○ ○ ○ ○ ○ ○ ○
	Sleep:	Z Z Z Z Z Z Z
	Energy Levels:	✦ ✦ ✦ ✦ ✦ ✦ ✦

Describe in detail what you got from doing today's self-care activity

_____

_____

_____

_____

_____

_____

_____

What would you like tomorrow to bring for you?

_____

_____

_____

Day Nineteen

Today's self-care activity:

How do you feel today?

What did today bring for you?

How did you deal with any challenges that came your way?

I am...	My Day	
	General mood:	☆ ☆ ☆ ☆ ☆
	Hydration:	○ ○ ○ ○ ○ ○ ○
	Sleep:	Z Z Z Z Z Z Z
	Energy Levels:	✚ ✚ ✚ ✚ ✚ ✚ ✚

Describe in detail what you got from doing today's self-care activity

_____

_____

_____

_____

_____

_____

_____

What would you like tomorrow to bring for you?

_____

_____

_____

_____

Day Twenty

Date: _____

Today's self-care activity: _____

How do you feel today?

_____

_____

_____

 What did today bring for you?

_____

_____

_____

_____

How did you deal with any challenges that came your way?

_____

_____

_____

_____

_____

I am...	My Day	
	General mood:	☆ ☆ ☆ ☆ ☆
	Hydration:	○ ○ ○ ○ ○ ○ ○
	Sleep:	Z Z Z Z Z Z Z
	Energy Levels:	✦ ✦ ✦ ✦ ✦ ✦ ✦

Describe in detail what you got from doing today's
self-care activity

_____

_____

_____

_____

_____

_____

_____

What would you like tomorrow to bring for you?

_____

_____

_____

_____

Day Twenty-One

Date: _____

Today's self-care activity: _____

How do you feel today?

What did today bring for you?

_____

_____

_____

_____

How did you deal with any challenges that came your way?

_____

_____

_____

_____

I am...	My Day	
	General mood:	☆ ☆ ☆ ☆ ☆
	Hydration:	○ ○ ○ ○ ○ ○ ○
	Sleep:	Z Z Z Z Z Z Z
	Energy Levels:	✚ ✚ ✚ ✚ ✚ ✚ ✚

Describe in detail what you got from doing today's self-care activity

_____

_____

_____

_____

_____

_____

_____

What would you like tomorrow to bring for you?

_____

_____

_____

_____

Day Twenty-Two

Date: _____

Today's self-care activity: _____

How do you feel today?

What did today bring for you?

_____

_____

_____

How did you deal with any challenges that came your way?

_____

_____

_____

_____

I am...	My Day	
	General mood:	☆ ☆ ☆ ☆ ☆
	Hydration:	○ ○ ○ ○ ○ ○ ○ ○
	Sleep:	Z Z Z Z Z Z Z
	Energy Levels:	✛ ✛ ✛ ✛ ✛ ✛ ✛ ✛

Describe in detail what you got from doing today's self-care activity

_____

_____

_____

_____

_____

_____

_____

What would you like tomorrow to bring for you?

_____

_____

_____

Day Twenty-Three

Today's self-care activity:

How do you feel today?

What did today bring for you?

How did you deal with any challenges that came your way?

I am...	My Day	
	General mood:	☆ ☆ ☆ ☆ ☆
	Hydration:	○ ○ ○ ○ ○ ○ ○
	Sleep:	Z Z Z Z Z Z Z
	Energy Levels:	✛ ✛ ✛ ✛ ✛ ✛ ✛

Describe in detail what you got from doing today's self-care activity

_____

_____

_____

_____

_____

_____

_____

What would you like tomorrow to bring for you?

_____

_____

_____

Day Twenty-Four

Date: _____

Today's self-care activity: _____

How do you feel today?

_____
_____
_____
_____

 What did today bring for you?

_____
_____
_____
_____

How did you deal with any challenges that came your way?

_____
_____
_____
_____

I am...	My Day	
	General mood:	☆ ☆ ☆ ☆ ☆
	Hydration:	○ ○ ○ ○ ○ ○ ○ ○
	Sleep:	Z Z Z Z Z Z Z
	Energy Levels:	✛ ✛ ✛ ✛ ✛ ✛ ✛

Describe in detail what you got from doing today's
self-care activity

_____

_____

_____

_____

_____

_____

_____

What would you like tomorrow to bring for you?

_____

_____

_____

Day Twenty-Five Date:

Today's self-care activity:

How do you feel today?

What did today bring for you?

How did you deal with any challenges that came your way?

I am...	My Day	
	General mood:	☆ ☆ ☆ ☆ ☆
	Hydration:	○ ○ ○ ○ ○ ○ ○ ○
	Sleep:	Z Z Z Z Z Z Z
	Energy Levels:	✛ ✛ ✛ ✛ ✛ ✛ ✛ ✛

Describe in detail what you got from doing today's
self-care activity

_____

_____

_____

_____

_____

_____

_____

What would you like tomorrow to bring for you?

_____

_____

_____

Day Twenty-Six

Date:

Today's self-care activity:

How do you feel today?

 What did today bring for you?

How did you deal with any challenges that came your way?

I am...	My Day	
	General mood:	☆ ☆ ☆ ☆ ☆
	Hydration:	○ ○ ○ ○ ○ ○ ○ ○
	Sleep:	ZZZZZZZ
	Energy Levels:	✚✚✚✚✚✚✚✚

Describe in detail what you got from doing today's self-care activity

_____

_____

_____

_____

_____

_____

What would you like tomorrow to bring for you?

_____

_____

_____

Day Twenty-Seven

Date: _____

Today's self-care activity: _____

How do you feel today?

_____

_____

_____

 What did today bring for you?

_____

_____

_____

_____

How did you deal with any challenges that came your way?

_____

_____

_____

_____

I am...	My Day	
	General mood:	☆ ☆ ☆ ☆ ☆
	Hydration:	○ ○ ○ ○ ○ ○ ○
	Sleep:	ZZZZZZZ
	Energy Levels:	✛ ✛ ✛ ✛ ✛ ✛ ✛

Describe in detail what you got from doing today's self-care activity

_____

_____

_____

_____

_____

_____

_____

What would you like tomorrow to bring for you?

_____

_____

_____

Day Twenty-Eight

Date: _____

Today's self-care activity: _____

How do you feel today?

 What did today bring for you?

How did you deal with any challenges that came your way?

I am...	My Day	
	General mood:	☆ ☆ ☆ ☆ ☆
	Hydration:	○ ○ ○ ○ ○ ○ ○
	Sleep:	ZZZZZZZ
	Energy Levels:	✛ ✛ ✛ ✛ ✛ ✛ ✛

Describe in detail what you got from doing today's self-care activity

_____

_____

_____

_____

_____

_____

_____

What would you like tomorrow to bring for you?

_____

_____

_____

Day Twenty-Nine

Date: ....

Today's self-care activity: ....

How do you feel today?

What did today bring for you?

_____

_____

_____

_____

How did you deal with any challenges that came your way?

_____

_____

_____

_____

I am...	My Day	
	General mood:	☆ ☆ ☆ ☆ ☆
	Hydration:	○ ○ ○ ○ ○ ○ ○ ○
	Sleep:	Z Z Z Z Z Z Z
	Energy Levels:	✛ ✛ ✛ ✛ ✛ ✛ ✛

Describe in detail what you got from doing today's
self-care activity

_____

_____

_____

_____

_____

_____

_____

What would you like tomorrow to bring for you?

_____

_____

_____

Day Thirty

Today's self-care activity:

How do you feel today?

 What did today bring for you?

How did you deal with any challenges that came your way?

I am...	My Day	
	General mood:	☆ ☆ ☆ ☆ ☆
	Hydration:	○ ○ ○ ○ ○ ○ ○
	Sleep:	Z Z Z Z Z Z Z
	Energy Levels:	✛ ✛ ✛ ✛ ✛ ✛ ✛

Describe in detail what you got from doing today's
self-care activity

_____

_____

_____

_____

_____

_____

_____

What would you like tomorrow to bring for you?

_____

_____

_____

_____

Thirty Day Review

Date: _____

Right now I feel: _____

How do you feel about your 30 days of self-care?

_____
_____
_____

What did you learn from the past 30 days?

_____

_____

_____

How did you deal with any challenges that came your way?

_____

_____

_____

_____

I Can...	My 30 Days	
	Overall mood:	☆ ☆ ☆ ☆ ☆
	Hydration:	○ ○ ○ ○ ○ ○ ○ ○
	Sleep:	ZZZZZZZ
	Energy Levels:	✦ ✦ ✦ ✦ ✦ ✦ ✦ ✦

Describe in detail what you think has improved for you over the past 30 days (if nothing, think about why not)

_____

_____

_____

_____

_____

_____

_____

What will you take away from your 30 days of self-care?

_____

_____

_____

_____

Date: _____

Notes

Notes

Date:

Date: _____   # Notes

Made in the USA
Columbia, SC
08 December 2022

73000597R00041